The COURTSHIP of SEA CREATURES

The COURTSHIP of SEA CREATURES

JEAN-PIERRE OTTE

translated from the French by
Marjolijn de Jager

GEORGE BRAZILLER / PUBLISHER
New York

Originally published in France under the title *La Sexualité d'un plateau de fruits de mer* by Éditions Julliard in 2000

First published in the United States of America in 2001 by George Braziller, Inc.

Copyright © 2000 by Éditions Julliard

English translation copyright © 2000 by George Braziller, Inc.

For information, please address the publisher:

George Braziller, Inc.
171 Madison Avenue
New York, NY 10016

Library of Congress Cataloging-in-Publication Data:

Otte, Jean Pierre, 1949–
[Sexualité d'un plateau de fruits de mer. English]
The courtship of sea creatures / Jean-Pierre Otte ; translated from the French by Marjolijn de Jager.
p. cm.
ISBN 0-8076-1486-6
I. Marine animals—Behavior. 2. Sexual behavior in animals. 3. Marine algae—Reproduction. I. Title.

QL121.O8813 2001
591.77—dc21   00-065099

Design by Rita Lascaro

Printed and bound in the United States of America

FIRST EDITION

For Bonbon
and her seafood

CONTENTS

"I was a star fallen into the sea,
octopus, sea urchin, and salmon,
seaweed moved only by
current and waves,
passing through all these transformations
to liberate myself at last,
to encounter the idea,
the desire for freedom
this art bestows."

—J.-P. Otte

I WAS ABOUT TO MAKE THE WISE, HEROIC DECISION OF going back to bed and waiting for the depression, of which I was the focal point, to lift on its own. Passing Minna's desk, I took her by surprise as she was hanging up the phone. I had the fleeting impression that I had caught her in an act of conspiracy, and I was not mistaken.

We all have these moments of eclipse, of passing through a void. Not much appears to be happening, but in our inner selves, in a private space inaccessible to us, minuscule changes are taking place that, in the end as they accumulate, constitute an inner event. What is generally called despondency or depression in retrospect seems like a sheltered state, a moment of retreat before a new blossoming. This does not take away from the fact that during these periods of indeterminate length one is difficult to live with, suffering without quite knowing why, continuously burdened by oneself and burdensome to others.

Minna was watching me with a sly and triumphant little smile, the messenger of an impromptu solution: I was being shipped off to the seashore! She had just discussed this at length with Anne-Charlotte, a friend, who was a school librarian in Rennes and who had a house at the ocean. That was of particular importance: the fisherman's cabin, built of granite, facing the forcefulness of the waves. The sea air, which is said to be invigorating, could certainly do me no harm. Heaven, or its executors, was coming to the aid of the disenchanted pilgrim. It was the end of my circling like a ragged, grimy wolf in his cage, observing with a vacant stare the sexual pursuit and copulation of beetles behind the dirty panes and bars of my terrariums. I was going to endure my pain elsewhere, long enough to recuperate, so to speak.

At the time I felt content, grateful that someone was making a decision for me, even though I was a bit taken aback by the zealousness with which I was being pushed out. The next evening there I was, stepping out of a bus in Brittany, my feet right in the middle of a puddle created by a recent downpour. With the irritating sound of water squelching in my boots, I headed for the fish store at the port where the key had been left. It was closing time; they were scrubbing the tiles and hosing them down, sweeping up scraps of ice, shells, and scales. The pungent smells vaguely awakened the memory of former whims, while the fishmongers—women—with their ice-cold, pink-marbled skin looked to me like nurses in a hospital somewhere beyond the Arctic Circle.

With the key in the palm of one hand and my suitcase in the other, I went toward the sea to meet this unknown mistress, immense and capricious, with whom I would have to live for an undetermined period of time, a stay of which in principle I myself was to decide the outcome.

Weighted by the night, the sea was black, even blacker than the night, shot through with rows of white crests, lines of foam emerging from the depths, running aground on the shore. A rustling noise arose from the coast penetrating the darkness, as if a beach stroller's two large seashells had been placed over my ears.

Although muted, the sound reverberated in Anne-Charlotte's house, where from the outset I sniffed a rather unpleasant and indefinable odor, dank and rancid, which I found hard to distinguish as that of a deserted house or of a young woman who no longer had lovers. I didn't recall the features of this friend of Minna's, though she had spent several days with us at one point. True, at the time I was busy day and night observing the delicate love life of leeches, catching them unawares, not yet thinking of experimenting in certain strategies and rather voluptuous fondlings with consenting partners of my own species.

The first night, I, who never dream or rarely remember doing so, had some dreams of tentacles, my legs entwined with slimy seaweed or with I know not what sucker-padded limbs, only to wake up with the sensation of a sticky kiss on the mouth, my body clammy beneath the channels of a bulging eiderdown.

The day was growing lighter through the windowpanes. Hurriedly dressing, I went out to meet the sea. Everything was vast, immoderate, freshly washed. The sky was glittering, revealing all of its depth beneath streaks of blue. Perspective fled at the horizon, where the white folds of the waves curved up in tilting and distant jubilation.

On the beach, the few rare strollers, up as early as I, seemed fixed in silence, lost by themselves and distant from one another in an undefined substance of emptiness and immensity. Under the steadily widening light, the streaks imprinted in the sand, the seaweed thrown down by the waves, were creating an embossed design, jointed like some large primitive script.

The moist wind, coming from the outermost bounds, in a constant shimmer, was tightening my features with invisible bands of salt. Above the reefs, the wind made the seagulls whirl under its lash in choreographic disorder. It seemed as if my face were nothing more than a transparent parenthesis. I had the impression of being a minuscule part of the world, a pathetic glimmer after all, but one that was a participant in both the infinity of beings and of things.

Strong and astringent, the air was making me drunk as it purified my lungs and forced me to breathe more deeply. Intoxicated, with glassy eyes, and suddenly with more space within, I went home to make myself a cup of Chinese black tea.

A life lived inside a shell, even in the proximity of the ocean, is not exempt from certain occupations. They are indeed sanctioned as if, from one end of the passage to the other, daily rituals and constant work might constitute a rappelling rope, a series of markers, and a thread thrown into the labyrinth all at the same time. Like a transcribing monk, Benedictine in his hours, I continued to copy creation myths (it was the period when I was working on the *Aubes enchantées*). Bent over primordial events, it seemed to me in a baffling way that, ahead of time, I was holding their reflection, their imprint, or their echo inside me. No doubt, there is nothing better than a creation myth to re-create oneself; at least, therein lies an invitation to living anew, the opportunity for a new beginning.

At low tide, beneath the silvery flight of seagulls going back up the estuary, I would return to the shore. I would pick up the treasures thrown down by the waves: razor shells, hollowed cockles, sea urchin spines, broken pieces of porcelain, the scattered gemstones of a piece of barbaric jewelry, a primitive adornment, or some coin. I would examine all of this with great care but never take anything home, perhaps hoping that one morning or evening there would be a seashell in a shape never before seen, an intriguing puzzle to be solved for oneself alone. The whorl emptying inside the shells became an outstanding meditative motif: a series of revolutions, through which time and space became combined to the point of merging.

Then I would move on to the inlets of the wild coast. In the large transparent pools, left in the rocks by the sea, rapture awaited me. Secluded until the next tide, lakes hung suspended in the middle of miniature mountains as in a Japanese water garden. The colors were enchanting, mixing ochers and umbers, tones of rust, Veronese green, various shades of pink and gray, and a burst of egg-yolk yellow scalloped by lichens.

I would crouch down to observe the sea anemones, barnacles, the sea urchins gathered together on the bottom like a group of chestnuts, and frenzied threadlike creatures, of an off-center or radial symmetry, endowed with swimming cilia, nameless larvae, dancing in a transparent alphabet soup in the pure inebriation of being alive. One day I surprised a little cuttlefish that had been careless enough not to withdraw with the tide; hidden in the darkness, it looked at me with a tender eye, frightened, dilated with an expression one might have called "feminine," all the while gracefully moving its slow tentacles, brought together like a crown above its head.

Delightfully reeling with the smells of the sea, I slid my fingers through the watery window, penetrating into another world, instinctively holding my breath. Crabs had entrenched themselves inside crevices set with mica; I tried to dislodge them, scaring them in order to understand their rituals of defense, their behavior when faced with danger. One of them pinched me savagely until I bled, but I didn't hold it against him: the risks of our encounter were shared.

Like all species and every individual of each species, this crab had his world in the world. I followed his diagonal advance with my gaze, but what view did he have of me? How was he seeing me, other than as a menacing and predatory shadow in the picture, surely?

One entire afternoon, I played with a sea anemone, slipping my fingers between the sleek and silky tentacles, feeling their heedful retraction. Thus I regained a sensitivity that had been diluted, as it were. When filled with wonder, one always opens up again to the universe and at the same time to one's own universe. Almost unconsciously I was recording the life rituals, tactics, appetites, and characteristics of the inhabitants of this ocean, which remains for us always, in its cycle of tides, the primitive ocean.

Private Secretions

S ea urchins enjoy being in large numbers, congregating in the sea, attached to the rocky bottom or half ensconced in the recesses they themselves have dug. They can be seen beneath the windows of the waves, gathered in fellowship, in colloquia, silent, placid, and almost motionless. Lost together and in groups, they seem to ignore each other without caring to maintain an equal distance among themselves. You might call them a state council of fat chestnuts or of perfectly round hedgehogs, resplendent in their spheres of ever-moving spines. It's enough to say that they exist in an indifferent promiscuity.

Each one is formed from a hard shell, of which I have a fossilized specimen tattooed with rust on my table, and sometimes my gaze or hand moves toward it, inadvertently as much as in the security of a kind of talisman.

The shell has five narrow sections, laid out like a star,

pierced with an infinity of channels through which pass moving organs, called "ambulacra," which act as extensions in a system of suckers. The creature stretches them out and retracts them at will quite nimbly in order to move and roll along the bottom.

This large nectarine shape is enveloped and bristly with moving spines—a fur of long thorns, fine mauve-green daggers—that give him protection, a permanent safeguard against the formidable jaws that wander around in the currents, against the perils and traps hidden among the underwater shadows.

When you are a sea urchin, you display your anus impudently on your upper side, as a keystone, at the center of five equal plates where the genital openings reside. The mouth is at the opposite pole on the lower side, directed toward the ground and armed with five protruding teeth, known as "Aristotle's lanterns," which serve as much for tearing apart prey, mollusks, or branches of kelp, as for digging its shelter in the rock.

The number five, which occurs constantly in the animal's composition, in symbolism is the number of the center, of harmony, of symmetry, and of balance. It is the symbol of the universe in which two axes, one vertical and the other horizontal, cross each other and pass through the center. It is the coat of arms of the five senses, the five primary colors, the five perceptible forms of matter. A five-pointed star, the sea urchin has five parts arranged around an axis like spokes around a hub, radiating out.

During the time of love—or what takes its place for them—when the genitals grow heated and the private substances start to bubble like the liquids in a still, the sea urchins, always close, don't dream of coming any closer. Without moving, they stay riveted to the spot, crouched beneath the slow swell of their spines. They continue to ignore each other, even if they feel an unusual trembling encompassing them, a fire that dilates their fibers like an instant of momentary glory or of wild terror.

Males and females, indistinguishable from the outside, reach sexual maturity at the same time, undoubtedly under the influence of the intensity of the growing light, the variation of temperature, or the return of the crescent moon.

Suddenly the moment is there, propitious, unquestionable, and irreversible. In a mad rush, the females are the first to liberate their gametes. And then the neighboring males immediately set their semen free, carried away by an implacable mimicry, a conditioned reflex, or a chain reaction to the emotion felt when they perceive the female secretions.

The currents, the oscillation of the waves, and the incessant movement of the protective spines will toss these gametes around to circulate freely within the group, and fertilization will be achieved haphazardly. We shall come back to these chance births, but first we must ponder the pleasure males and females do or do not experience in the secretion. Nothing allows for confirmation and supposition of, indeed hope for, this, as if the sure, excessive, and dazzling pleasure other species feel in the love act should have an origin. The evolution would start, so to speak, with an archaic enjoyment, a rudimentary delight in the primitive ocean out of which life and all its constantly multiplied and inventive life-forms came. One can believe in a crude and simple euphoria in the robust enterprise of propagation, self-expression, the discharging of one's organs, and the ejection of one's seed.

Gametes, through a sequence of accidents in the currents, in meeting, uniting or fusing, will form the embryos. Fertilization is facilitated by the number of urchins that live together, by the quantity of the reproductive substances secreted, but also and especially by the presence of a chemical substance in the ovum's envelope, which attracts the spermatozoa like a magnet, like an irresistible call.

The fact remains that the predominant role of chance in these encounters leaves us disconcerted, dumbfounded, perhaps even suspicious or nostalgic. For, in the end, faced with the uncertainty of what is possible, one cannot prevent oneself from dreaming of the generations that might have been born in place of those selected by the whims of the waves.

At the end of three or four weeks, ciliated larvae come out of the eggs. They spin around and around and swim in frail feverishness, part of the plankton, suspended as if between two periods of time. They seem like nearly transparent, dancing, whirling particles until, through the larva's transformation, the sea urchin is formed, at first only as big as the head of a pin, but open to every hope of flourishing, to the fortuitous events of the unknown future.

The Tentacular Embrace

The eye of the cuttlefish is terrible, pensive, profound: as you look at her you realize that you are being observed at the same time. In its huge engulfing eyes reflections of feeling appear that one might call almost human, expressions of fleeting astonishment or dread, until a strange and placid heaviness overtakes the pupils, dully dilating them inside the white.

The head is embellished with ten very flexible and quick tentacles, covered with suckers along their full length. Two of these arms are longer than the others and can be retracted at will, each with a bulbous bud at its end equipped with suckers. A little girl, who was observing it with me, said that "a cuttlefish wears its legs around a mouth," leaving it up to you to decide whether it's waiting to be kissed or tempted to bite.

The mouth juts far out in front of a body shaped like an

elongated and sleek sack. Its coat of muscular fabric is edged with a fringed membrane that acts like a undulating fin.

Beneath the throat, a slit leads to a wide bronchial cavity, placed like an apron-bib pocket where the water rushes in and then escapes through a kind of funnel. By suddenly contracting the sides of this funnel and roughly pushing out the water that inflates it, the animal manages to propel itself resolutely, although in a backward direction.

This possibility of fleeing backward and in spurts is one of several means of personal protection. The cuttlefish, by adopting an ambiguous coloring, can instantaneously match its surroundings, varying its color and blending in with the rocky or sandy background. Still blending in, with an imperceptible undulation of its swimming fringe, nearly invisible at this point, she approaches her prey.

When greater danger threatens, the cuttlefish ejects a blackish brown liquid from its funnel, a cumulus cloud of opaque ink aggressively darkening the water, thereby hiding from the eye of the predator, which had placed its hopes on the little creature to satisfy its appetite. Dumbfounded and intensely irritated, it now finds itself caught in the sepia of artists without having any creative talent.

After having emptied all its ink in order to slip away, the cuttlefish goes back to its usual rituals and rhythms to continue its life elsewhere, most often near the shore. It burrows halfway into the sand, gives in to a nap or idle meditation, then coming out of its moment of indolence, it starts moving again, slowly swimming with apparent sensuality. It drifts toward its favorite pastures, feeds on fish and crustaceans, suddenly extending its two long tentacles when a prey passes within reach.

On the outside the animal is not covered with any shell whatsoever, but a hard strip, appropriately called the "cut-tlebone," lies in the dorsal region. We could surmise that, like a memory fragment, this is what is left of an original shell lost in evolution's wanderings. When at last the will to come out of its shell was affirmed, this bone was gradually *internalized* to become a skeleton, a stable and reliable arma-ture for a soft-fleshed creature.

The lights of the equinox grow more intense and produce fascinating and playful reflections, streaks of marbling in motion, mosaics of liquid gold in the depths. And at night the moon's brightness shimmers on the waves, scattering the stars of a fairy-tale world in the eddies of the foam's overflow. It is time to go to the site of the dances of love.

When you are a cuttlefish, you enjoy parades and nuptial waltzes. It is a slow and sumptuous choreography, filled with majesty and phantasmagoria. The partners, magnetized, pulled toward each other by an irresistible drive, lose con-sciousness of the dangers surrounding them, not thinking to eject their ink in order to spend an opaque night that would be theirs alone. Love in darkness has its advantages, how-ever, providing sensations that are like no other, an inde-scribable trembling as you outline your partner with gentle touches, sculpt with a patient, yet impatient palm, follow-ing the naked lines that come to haphazardly cross back and forth. But the cuttlefish has other sexual ambitions; in the dance it chooses to expose itself entirely to view and to take advantage of the lights embellishing its skin, draping it in a theatrical and bewitching substance.

Through the constant undulation of their fringed membranes, the swaying of their bodies, and a complicated and enchanting movement of their tentacles, they seek to seduce each other still more, brushing against each other and growing aroused by this accidental contact.

At times their waltz has something macabre about it, at times it is marvelous and lyrical. Sometimes the male rises up as a figure of dread, his only purpose to submit the fiancée of the moment to his desires, to obtain her consent through terror, while she, full of grace and with fluid freedom, evokes a look of candor or tactical shyness, meant both to bewitch her partner more intimately and to increase the courage of his virility. At the same time, she would like to calm a last fear as she nears the act she still somewhat confusedly desires, now sensing that she has been seduced. In any case, her manner invites a slow progression in their relationship.

There they are, beginning to touch each other lightly and in their trembling to flutter and brush against each other at length, no longer by accident but in the boldness of a new and undefined pleasure. They come even closer, rub up against each other, twist in vibration, begin to intertwine their tentacles in all kinds of prolonged, multiple, and varied fondlings, which are then repeated with solemn persistence, perturbed by the reverberation the experience arouses in the depth of their being.

One never has arms enough for loving and embracing, and cuttlefish, like true little goddesses of Siva, can only congratulate themselves on having so many tentacles with which to entwine and explore each other's most sensitive areas in a series of swaying, diffused, encircling motions that finally mingle, merge, and glow in the progressive embrace.

The extreme sensual delight lies perhaps in the subtle play of suckers coming together, moving apart, connecting again gently on a bubble of air, and provoking a sense of dizziness and vertigo, a heightening of the senses with each new movement. In any event, the maneuvers prove to be effective in awakening all their molecules to the act of love. Enraptured, the cuttlefish look deeply into each other's eyes, yet it doesn't occur to them to use their mouths for a kiss or a delicious nibble.

Copulation is achieved through progressive glides, a prolonging of their foreplay. Swimming slowly in place, their fins swaying like the hem of a dress in the wind, cuttlefish hold each other suspended in their embrace, between two currents, between two intervals of time, contemplative, solemn, wholly devoted to the endeavor of joining.

From among his tentacles the male disengages one that has grown swollen for the occasion, as if the ardor and importance of the procedure should, in the eyes of the female, always be expressed by the quality of an expert and distended muscle. It is with this arm, for lack of a penis or any other tool, that he will extract the spermatozoa from his ventral cavity to then bury them in his partner's cavity with no further ado, with a confident gesture as if nimbly guided by her.

This form of copulation is the same as that of similar species, the squid and octopus. But with the so-called argonaut octopus, found in the Mediterranean, there is an additional step to the exploit, a dramatic turn of events, an amputation that leaves one amazed and demands morbid admiration.

First, we shall describe the female as she waits for love. She has made herself beautiful, attractive, full of grace, carrying a false shell of luxurious, waving fabric in the form of a very slender cradle, not attached to the mantle but supported and guarded by two of her arms. The bride, awaiting her betrothed, worries that no one is coming. Swimming in the waves, impatient to be conquered and to conquer a body and a heart, she has had a hundred dreams of being delicately touched, subtly nibbled at, of pleasures impossible to define that will remain unfulfilled. She is justifiably alarmed that she will be left stranded.

At some distance, out of sight in any event, the male is accumulating a large amount of semen, surrounded by capsules called spermatophores, in his ventral cavity. He extracts this semen with one of his tentacles and then, as the author of *Physique de l'amour* put it, "this arm grows into a spatula, arms itself with a flagellum, loses its suckers, and then, when it is heavy with life like a ripe bunch of grapes, it separates, wanders toward the female, enters her belly, lodges in her pallial cavity, and forces the semen into her organs where it will encounter the ovula."

Thus, the male organ appears here as a temporary individual, a third being between father and mother, a messenger bringing the male's genital treasure to the female. Neither one knows or will ever know the other. The male knows nothing about the beauty for which he has sliced off a limb, and the female knows of her sire only the fertilizing organ. Obviously, there is something distressing and abrupt about this relationship, a great disappointment, a clash of all the subtle dreams of seduction, which the female undoubtably has no thought of lamenting. As it is impossible for her to imagine other ways of fulfilling her desire, she must make do with this.

Under the Sign of Pincers

*I*t is perhaps by sharing the life of a crab, deprived of a real copulatory tool, that one can best understand the convenience of acquiring a penis when, in the course of evolution, nature strove to endow partners with appropriate, easy, and pleasant instruments to manipulate under the sway of the greatest of desires.

To shield themselves from the currents and violent eddies that would carry them off into the open sea, crabs lodge in the cavities of rocks, in the crevices and rifts spotted with lichens, seaweed, and bits of shell uncovered by the retreating sea. With every ebb tide, they disembark once again in a world of reefs and strands where their reference points, their paths, and their rituals lie.

The wind and sun dry their shells, and their lungs—forced open by breathing the air—expand with a vehement cry that pulls them toward the shore by unseen ties that are the ties of salt and blood, the urgency of appetites and permanent conflicts.

In the distance, without diminishing the mystery that enlivens it so magnificently, the sea unfolds like a huge fringed wing, a mirror ceaselessly divided, ceaselessly reconstructed beneath the starry sky. It swells with underwater forces as if another sea lies below this one; it rises up and covers the previous wave with foam. But as soon as it has expanded, it withdraws even farther, like the sleeper who wakes up in a dream clutching tangled sheets. The shore is completely unveiled, with its shimmerings, its seaweed torn loose from the depths, the scattered round of seashells, hollow razor shells, and the spines of sea urchins.

Such harshness! Such vast air on the contours of the newly emerged world where crabs dare to venture, their heads suffused by noise. Seagulls hurl metal-sharp cries, and salt, like hoar frost, outlines skeletal feet and pincers.

Beneath a greenish hue that appears lacquered, each one shows a highly developed cephalothorax from which radiate five pairs of thoracic legs, only the first pair of which is equipped with formidable pincers. The mouth, armed with chewing parts, lies on the ventral side, in front of a flat, triangular, and undeveloped abdomen. It does not need to play the role of an organ of propulsion in a philandering animal, moving sideways at a decent speed on an oblique path.

In order to attain this size and to aspire to more ambitious dimensions, the crab must undergo a series of changes.

The larva, as tiny as the head of a pin and whirling about, presents an unusual and even extravagant appearance, its head with a long rostrum and a kind of frontal horn tilted backward like the crested hairstyle of the punk era. Next it undergoes its metamorphosis and, although extremely tiny, becomes a complete and perfect crab of a translucent and grayish substance that conceals it in the transparent worlds of the sea.

How else to evolve and grow beneath a shell unless by passing through a series of sheddings, of which not enough has been said given the incredible effort and the tearing and painful duress they require each time.

A few hours before the operation begins, the crab rubs his feet against each other and, without changing location, moves each one of them in turn. He turns over on his back and seems to contract as he concentrates all his strength at the point where his muscles meet, and then he suddenly relaxes, while his feet and pincers move in continuous vibration. These movements give the various parts of the body a little play within their sheaths. After these preliminaries, the crab inflates his body more than usual, in an excess of audacity and ambition or in an implacable and irreversible stage of growth. The part of the shell that lies between thorax and the first ring of the abdomen is the first to be torn and give way: the body juts out, covered with the new, soft coating.

Having reached this point, the crab rests for a while, granting himself some respite by releasing the tension, only to gather his strength again and muster his headstrong will. The agitation of the feet and the body's vibration begin all over again. The shell is forced up and forward by the body's emergence and remains attached only in the oral region. Pulled backward, the head extricates itself halfway, and the eyes free themselves of the old coating as of a pillowcase. The feet try to release themselves, and a slit is produced in the earlier covering, making the operation easier. Then the crab's head emerges completely with an impatient movement full of energy and pride, and he allows himself another rest. One last time, he gathers his spirit and strength and with an abrupt thrust, a jump with which to join the new present, a leap into the immediate future, he abandons the former exterior skeleton that served him as ornament and protection.

Worn out from this series of lacerations and heroic efforts, the crab remains weak after the molting process. All his feet are so soft that, in the air, especially around the joints, they fold and shake like twists of wet paper. He will have to wait several hours and the return of the tide before his locomotive organs firm up. Then he begins his course again, always sideways and at a slant, on the world's diagonal, carried by a new mood, his appetite stimulated by a burning hollow in his abdomen.

It is precisely in their appetite that crabs show themselves to be in a bellicose mood, inflexible, fierce, entrenched in alert awareness and rugged self-dignity. They get into murderous fights over nothing, a seashell to be bickered about, bothered especially by the presence of the other, the second self, the counterpart, like an annoying reflection in the mirror. Carapace against carapace, they knock into and attack each other cruelly with their pincers, give each other mortal blows, straddle and gut each other, even devouring each other, intent on delivering the intruder to their gastric juices, but at the same time being devoured by him. They reduce each other to nothing or almost nothing: two gashed and empty shells to be collected by the next tide.

However, in the battle they enjoy an astonishing characteristic that all of the earth's invalid veterans and amputees would envy. When they feel caught in the adversary's pincers, they have the ability to break off their limbs, to amputate themselves in a way, through a lightning-quick, dynamic contraction of the muscles. And the marvel is that those lost limbs, left in the hands of the conqueror, waste no time in growing back. After the battle, the crab regenerates. Intact, with a perfectly restored body and his aggressiveness unchecked, he ventures forth again toward new amoral tournaments, since a war with rules would be merely a social game.

Fortunately, love among crabs is not accompanied by any ablation and does not assume a combative aspect, even if the male, immediately or almost, displays a sovereign, authoritarian, and imperious desire that does not brook much resistance.

The female disseminates molecules of a ripe and harrowing odor to the wind, which the male captures—to a point of intoxication—wherever his wanderings take him. These erratic scents assure him that she is in the best of moods as he feels in his lower abdomen the stirring of his own readiness to mate, a fierce desire, and, as it were, a challenge to his virility.

In his approach he becomes music-mad. He uses his carapace, rubbing and banging it against stones or hollow shells in order to produce songs that John Cage would have appreciated. These shocks, persistent gratings, these beats, sometimes hollow and sometimes resonant, set the rhythm for his project.

As soon as he notices the unknown female, who could just as easily be any other unknown, beloved in advance, he begins to pitch signals. By lifting and weirdly turning his pincers, he initiates a chat that certainly includes some aesthetic ceremonial outbursts but, above all, provides them with a language only they understand. It serves as a kind of semaphore for sending greetings first, before, all at the same time and in a disorderly fashion, flaunting his arguments, other urgent appeals, as well as the narrative of his past and future exploits. Finally, the female responds with less assertive signs, shy or hesitant, while, from a private burning of the abdomen, feelings of sudden apprehension rise up in her, the cold outlines of a last bit of fear.

All around them the sea shimmers, seagulls screech their sharp cries, the foam flattens its edges in a white rustling of washing water. The close and far-off sounds make their senses spin now that the signaling has stopped and the partners, disconcerted, size up each other in tactical immobility or pause before the amorous assault. Suddenly, the grayish shadow of a crab-eating heron slides across the sand, and together they will justifiably seek refuge in a crevice. The embrace will take place in the shade, in a sudden bluish coolness, saturated with the smell of rotten seaweed and fish.

To mate, the male clambers onto his beloved from the side before he straddles her. The semen oozes from the lower part of his body, and since he has no copulatory tool whatsoever, he will draw it out with one of his feet hollowed like a drainpipe. With a difficult motion, a clumsy contortion at first, he then brings the semen to the genital orifices of his submissive fiancée, silent throughout the performance.

This is a kind of stage, a transitional wandering or a ludicrous digression, that, in a spirit of expedient accommodation, later on led nature to the invention of the penis by which new species were to profit, without thought of complaining.

Love in a Colony

Mussels live in colonies on rocky coasts among other colonies of barnacles, limpets, murices, sea anemones, or winkles. These species, with different characteristics and appetites, share the same territories, coexist without harming each other, without trying to pick fights, and even without setting boundaries among themselves: they mingle but always in scattered groups of the same kind.

There is no doubt that in an indifferent happiness, in compromise or peaceful coalition, every species, indeed every individual of every species, is distinguishable through a group of specific constants, characteristics, and aptitudes, in a similar pleasure of being alive, here and now. All of them obey the great primitive rhythms of the tides: they close, they cloister themselves in their own shadows, and then they reopen when the waves, breaking on the reefs and in the cavities with a magnificent roaring and splashing, return.

It is not easy to decide whether or not there is social organization in every mussel bed. Perhaps it is more appropriate to speak of a kind of anarchy, haphazardly and naturally organized, where things are communicated without there being any need for a means of communication. When we are preoccupied to the point of obsession with protection, welfare, and security, it is hard to approach the idea of a form of anarchy that nevertheless leads to harmony. It is even harder to understand and accept this. Does not becoming socially organized always mean replacing a natural order, being enclosed in an artificial media-created world without truly being in the world any longer? Some earlier minds have recently allowed themselves to be perturbed by this cluster of contradictory ideas and even, with a last bit of precaution, allowed a desire to overtake them, which accepting these ideas may well increase. Perhaps, then, it is time to be open to greater audacity and invention, rediscovering the laws of origin, by which things become organized and communicate on their own without any need to organize them.

Things grow complicated and are clarified amid even greater confusion in the case of the mussel that leads a sometimes wandering, sometimes fixed existence. She puts her foot outside her shell and moves around in a skulking mood. Perhaps capable of wonder, she roams the depths, makes excursions inspired more by nomadic curiosity than by appetite, always ending her journey by catching up with herself, or almost. She comes back to settle in the same place or elsewhere, comes back to breathe in company because that's her nature, comes home to the cluster, the gathered group in tiers.

To settle down, she elegantly stretches out her foot on the rocky brace, depositing a viscous secretion, a kind of glue, and then stretching this into filaments called byssus. The mussels cling and stick to each other in groups, as they cut the threads that hold them to the rock and to the others and then pick up their wanderer's existence again, drunk with the unknown and other unknowns.

The shell around her comes from the inner depth of the mussel herself. It is like the exteriorization or the perfect manifestation of an inner motive: it is secreted. The egg gives birth to a planktonic larva, wreathed with a ciliated crown that allows it to swim, or more precisely, to wriggle in fragile feverishness. Most of the time, these larvae float on the surface of the sea while the shell they excrete is formed. The translucent fabric of these minuscule larvae, looking more like the letters of some mysterious constantly moving alphabet, produces a substance made by the extraordinary efforts of an internal distillery. Gradually, this sketch of a shell hardens, begins to have some weight, and soon drags them to the deep where the complex transformations of the metamorphosis continue.

Then the mussel can consider herself lucky for the accomplishment of having a shell that protects her quite well (except from the pincers of a crab), encloses her in a solitude belonging to her alone, and, isolates her perfectly within the promiscuity of the cluster. This shell is made up of two valves, fused by a horned hinge, which two contracting muscles close tightly with stubborn determination.

The body wears a coat of a moist and attractive yellow ocher, which hides the branchiae and shelters the visceral mass continued in the foot, which she projects to move herself as easily as others stick out the tip of their tongue. She lives inside her shell, in the heart of a wet and oblong darkness, always lying on her side, immersed in an undefined somnolence, perhaps embellished by a few lazy dreams when she is closed.

If she is not disturbed, the mussel half opens with an ever new voluptuousness, especially when satisfying her appetites. The mouth lies in the area of the hinge, equipped with four feelers covered with cilia, and she rapidly moves the branchiae, equally supplied with cilia, to make the water circulate inside her shell, constantly filtering it and holding on to the plankton that nourish her.

Furthermore, you can only be delighted with the pleasure you'd take when enfolded by those cilia and that foot, playing like an entirely knowledgeable and expert tongue. These refined tools, of a sure and subtle eroticism, could only produce indescribable sensations and leave the intense desire in your memory to re-create them as soon as possible. It is a great disappointment to learn that inside a mussel bed no embrace whatsoever takes place. To any more or less bold and successful form of mating, each one of them prefers the privilege of its solitude, a quality of isolation within the cloister of its shell, a complete absence of contact that has the saline flavor of the absolute.

Their sexuality awakens at the same time or in very quick succession, as if they needed to catch up on some delay, influenced certainly by light and a sudden increase in heat that is communicated to their molecules and shakes them up without their thinking of normal appetites any more. Most often this occurs at the rising tide before or just after the summer solstice. Time is undefined and vast, but suddenly the moment is there, imposing itself as propitious, inescapable, and supreme.

The male mussels are the first to discharge their gametes. It is a waltz of slender spermatic snakes, a network of liquid crystal threads. These threads are stretched and tangled; deformed by the currents, the filaments are quickly broken and haphazardly venture out, their destiny put into other invisible hands like a whitish script of arabesques. There is undoubtedly pleasure in the ejection; at least the pleasure of freeing and relieving themselves, of pouring out the seed that has glutted them to the point of bursting.

In contrast to their sea urchin sisters, the females do not cast out their gametes. Instead, they preserve them beneath their mantle, but incessantly and almost frenetically they do their utmost to make the cilia, covering their branchiae and labial feelers, vibrate in order to create circulation, a current that brings them the spermatic threads. Quite obviously, other filaments wander off and get lost in the vast space of the sea and in time, for lack of having encountered the other half that would allow them to reconstruct the unity of their origin.

Theirs has been called a primitive orgy. Still, it is a strange form of debauchery when they do not touch, when they abstain from any contact however slight its intimacy, when they never mix, when they never join bodies, and above all when they never even meet. If one were to speak of an orgy, it is limited solely to the gametes, anonymously delivered to the whims of currents and the long-hidden fingers of chance.

The Moist Secret

*a*ny experience with the sea is useless if it does not miraculously take us back to the universe of women and allow us, if not to understand them, at least to share their mysteries. That the oyster is an emblem, a coat of arms of the female, is obvious and borne out by our touch (timid and then insistent), and then our tasting.

More so than her partners, woman has preserved within her the great original rhythms, the oceanic and lunar cycles, the curving dance of seaweed, the secret life of seashells, and the very tentacles of the cuttlefish. In her flesh and even in her moods, she carries the variations of her feelings—always faithful to love, as much in its burning absence as in a fulfillment that bestows upon her skin a glow, a magnificent luster. Born from the waves, resonant with its wildest as well as its subtlest fluctuations, she has entered a religion of the wave. Her charms, which attract us, in respected, evolved and finally *personalized* forms, are changing fruits—like those of the sea—capricious, surging, expanding, then withdrawing like anemones at low tide, to come together, to close, and to be strengthened. Still, the sexual organ has no shell, and the true lover prefers it naked. There is no doubt that, side by side with the guild of hairdressers and barbers, a class should be created of experts in the intimate, perfect, and smooth shearing, of such moist sleekness that it penetrates the fingers. These underwater lips are bewitching, heartrending by the life that secretly excites them, both from a nostalgia for the origins and from what the Germans call *Sehnsucht*, a nostalgia for the future in which we ceaselessly become what we are.

The oyster, though, having to preserve itself from dangers and appetites that do not come under the heading of voluptuousness but under that of loss and bedlam, resides in a shell made of two unequal valves, one shaped like a cover and the other hollow to contain it.

A thick muscular band, that can be stretched and tightened at will, leaves it cloistered at low tide, half open at high tide. Whether they live communally in a cluster or in banks of considerable dimensions, each of them enjoys complete solitude inside its shell, a sure isolation, integrity, and constant journeymanship with itself. Its fears and excitements are not shared with anyone, although the others to which it is glued without doubt feel comparable fears and similar excitements.

As its coat does not have a single protruding foot, the
oyster is forever riveted, fixed, and sedentary by the tight
injunction of its nature. It always has the same vision of the
world, its world, or more precisely, the same viewpoint on
a universe that nevertheless is changing and varies with
the tides, the bursts of light, the atmospheric pressures or
depressions. In this it differs from the mussel, equipped
with the tool and mood necessary to keep it moving, clam-
bering the depths of the mud in excursions of discovery.
Yet, the oyster feeds in a similar way, opening halfway, agi-
tating the cilia that cover its labial feelers and its
branchiae to make the water circulate. The currents are
laden with the microscopic larvae of plankton, which it
filters to nourish itself. When you touch them with the tip
of your nail, these cilia quickly retract, and you cannot
help being moved by such an intimate mechanism working so marvelously, by the sudden flow of oily moisture,
which is proof of its extreme sensitivity.

With other mollusks and gastropods, the oyster shares
the privilege of an alternating hermaphroditism: either the
same organ is entirely transformed, being first male and
then female; or, divided into a male and a female hemi-
sphere, the two halves mature simultaneously or succes-
sively in order to be fertilized.

Inside its shelter, in its darkness and oily moisture, the
oyster surrenders to an almost circular turning in on itself,
to forgetting all else, to the carelessness of an idle and art-
ful life, liberated from ordinary imperatives and appetites,

which it must still satisfy, at the return of every tide, by reflex or in its daily routine of preservation.

Closed in on its secret in the strictest intimacy, it then seems to enjoy its double identity in the miracle of feeling so completely alive. It awakens to a mysterious, refined, and troubling existence in which tremblings seem to be the continuation of quickly vanished dreams. Contemplative, listening to itself, eager for its own sensations, it feels its organs stir. There are imperceptible vibrations, expansions it does not think of repressing, followed by withdrawals and effusions in its double self-embrace, that occur in the same space but at different times.

From September to May, oysters are male and develop sperm. From June onward, in the period indicated by the summer solstice, the ovaries mature, are swollen with whitish ova, which the spermatozoa, born in the preceding cycle and fully immersed in their role, take by storm.

Unknown to the world, this clandestine love and sexuality between the opposing parts of oneself, through which one is united in order to reproduce oneself in the secret and solitude of one's shell, are inscribed in the cells as an inevitable program and, more importantly still, appear as an imposed duty, a procedure from which they cannot possibly stray. But here as elsewhere, nature compensates without doubt, with an array of unprecedented sensations for the obligation of satisfying appetites, the scope of which goes beyond us.

The eggs open beneath the mantle in the dark moisture, and the oyster's final pleasure is to give itself, to expand by opening more than it normally does. The embryos, equipped with swimming cilia, disperse and form a whitish cloud. A milky matter, the spat, gets lost under the waves. The embryos swim and writhe in mad activity, frenetic and bizarre, drunk with life, drunk with venturing into an immense universe without limits, one might say, like a labyrinth of fluid windows, that appear and disappear, losing their silvering in inaccessible transparencies.

Only in their early infancy and for a very brief time, do the young oysters know the freedom of the road and of the hazardous excursion, as they give themselves over to games, as it were. After a few hours, a few days, they will attach themselves to a rock to become the large version of what in reduced size they already are, so marvelously complete.

*   *   *

Even though sexuality does not appear to play a role in its shaping, I would like to dwell for a moment on the pearl, for the fascinating and fertile image it provides of our own blossoming. Legends tell that it is born from the effect of lightning or from the fall of a dewdrop during moonlit nights: "The sacred shells receive in their silken mantles these precious nighttime tears and, in the sea's mystery, in the absolute solitude of the shells, pearls are formed, daughters of the heavens, fertilized by celestial seed . . . "

Confronted with these poetic origins, without agreeing with them, natural science more prosaically explains that the pearl is born from the invasion of a particularly sharp grain of sand that irritates and even cuts the mantle. Henry de Monfreid, who was a trafficker and magnificent pirate, spoke of a variety of skate fish that ejects a microscopic parasite in its excrement, a kind of acarus, which attaches itself to the oyster's flesh and penetrates it, bringing with it a part of the secretory mother-of-pearl epithelium that forms a cyst: the pearl.

In symbolism it becomes, all at the same time and like a mystical element, the sublimation of instincts, the spiritualization of matter, the transfiguration of the elements, and the shining end of an evolution in the glow of a pure mystery. It has also been said that there is a resemblance between the pearl and the fetus, there where I tend to see rather the formation of "the pleasure organ."

But what, in my eyes, is more important still is the scratch, the nick, as fine as it is deep, from a grain of sand or the invasion of a parasite. Perhaps therein lies a law, the secret of personal blossoming: a wound is the necessary precondition for all creation.

The Passion of Starlike Beings

O f all the species encountered, the starfish is the only one with an astounding variety of reproductive means at her disposal. True daughter of caprice, she can allow herself to give in instaneously to the most incongruous inspirations and whims, for her characteristics always give her the means, the opportunity, and the possibility of responding to them, no matter which intimate operation she has just chosen. Nature seems to have gone out of its way to assemble in her a profusion of procreative systems, at a stage of evolution when it had not yet decided to divide them among the species and to perfect them in the perspective of progress.

The echinoderm has a star-shaped body—symbolically this is once again a fascinating form of perfection, axes crossing inside a radiating symmetry. Its skin is pulpy, orange-hued or reddish, coated with chalky sediment, and strewn with appendages that look like thorns, while the yellowish-white underside of its arms is equipped with retractable ambulacra that pass through orifices. It is like a throng of minuscule legs, an army of cilia both firm and flexible, each one of which ends in a sucker like an oil droplet. All of this, emerging first in disorder, begins enigmatically to organize itself in the next stage, allowing the starfish both to move around and to settle by fastening expertly to the crevices and eroded rocks of the coast when the tide returns.

Reproducing its exterior appearance, the mouth, which is situated on the lower side, is star-shaped and immediately linked to the gastric space, which is extended through a short intestinal tract. The starfish has no intention of prolonging its digestion. Oysters and mussels are its favorite food. It opens the shells by bringing pressure to bear with its ambulacral feet, attaching itself through the play of its thousand suckers, which expand breaking the resistance of the interior closing muscles. Quickly and astonishingly it then swallows the oyster or the mussel whole, enveloping it with its stomach, which it devaginates and nimbly turns around outside its body only to bring it back in with a swift and supple suction movement. Right away, the prey is in the stomach as if the taste buds were placed in its inner lining among the oozing digestive juices.

The starfish inhales seawater through a madreporic plaque that, under a magnifying glass, looks like the knob of a watering can and sits at the base of one of its arms. Water irrigates it continuously and makes the locomotive ambu-lacra swell. All this occurs beneath a network of sensory points, cells that are especially sensitive to light and its vari-ations. These cells come together like grains of pigment in pointillist passion and make up a kind of primitive eye, in a nude blush that appears at the end of its arms.

If the sexual apparatus awakens only at certain times, by urgently warming and shaking the molecules, the idea of reproduction may nevertheless come to the starfish, by acci-dent or by caprice, at any time. They may begin to bud or have recourse to their exceptional faculties of regeneration.

This idea, almost a desire, undoubtedly crops up at moments of solitude, respite, or distraction, in a mood of idleness that is the mother of all extravagance, while they lie lazily in the sun without stirring a muscle or take refuge halfway into the bluish darkness of a crevice rid-dled with sea salt. No longer do they notice the sound of the waves, unless as background noise, so intensely pre-occupied are they with having to make a resolution, with having to break through a feeling of oppression. Outside of the obligation to satisfy your normal needs, you can't be happy when you constantly have to observe even the most subtle variations of light with just a rudimentary eye. Everything comes to an end. The joy of life turns intangibly into boredom, and disgust is born from growing accustomed to predilection and satiation. One must per-ish in life or be open to a new beginning, prepared to resort to invention.

Suddenly the starfish feel cramped, despite the vastness around them, as if each were judging its own life to be too large for itself alone and had the idea of dividing itself up as one divides up an apartment. Even more they feel the sense of a pathetic void, of a fruitless egoism, a solitude from which they could be liberated by exuberantly multiplying.

Already they are starting to swell, filled with a simmering of their own energy and an undefined effervescent matter, like the breakthrough of buds distending and splitting under the pressure of spring sap. It is an invisible force to which they submit, unable to do anything but submit and, lacking freedom, finding pleasure in acceptance and in the fever of the moment.

Then starfish choose to multiply by schizogenesis. Either they divide resolutely by autotomy, slicing themselves into two halves, each one of which will then reconstruct the other half. Or they relinquish one of their arms to the current, an arm they cut off through deliberate contraction of the muscles or in the adversity of a fight.

In the first scenario, it is as if the rudiments of physics and the metaphysics of the double, the second self, the equal, are found there: an identity, at least the sensation of an almost personal life, is to be found again in the identical. Twins appear who will not know each other, developing in their unique knowledge of the sea thanks to their sensory cells, as much in their period of nomadism as in their fixed existence. Each of the halves entrenches itself in the conspiring darkness of a crevice or hides beneath the curving dance of the seaweed to restore itself to its original form, to rediscover a previous state in the present and immediate future.

In the second scenario, the same pride in reconstituting its physical integrity is seen, the necessary and urgent desire to rediscover oneself whole, intact, after a fight that had left the starfish humiliated and mutilated.

A crab, in fact, takes one of the starfish's arms between its pincers, devours it on the spot without cleaning it of its spiky sediments and without worrying about being disturbed or spied on. Bite after bite with its chewing parts, it gobbles up the dish, which will be dissolved in the acidity of the gastric juices: the arm disappears in digestion. He is completely ignorant of the fact that, in truncated form and with the appearance of an amputated comet, the starfish is busy faithfully re-creating its lost limb as it continues to roam or find shelter. A new arm, just like the earlier one, could be shown to the crab's covetous eye.

If things were brought to a complete understanding, the crab would need to penetrate the secret of a conjuring session, to understand an occult privilege or a bizarre capability, a trick of substitution more difficult to digest, while he would continue to swallow what was growing back under his very eyes as he goes along.

Finally, love comes along, elating the starfish and expanding their senses when the great tide returns beneath the spell of the moon. With the maturation of the sexual cells, which swell considerably underneath the genital orifices placed all the way down the arms' extremities, desire or the drive for regeneration comes to them.

It is a long-distance love, a way of communicating that no longer offers us anything new, where males and females rid themselves of their gametes in the water, and fertilization takes place when these happen to meet wherever the currents take them. However, it is fitting to appreciate that these distant relationships spare them the often laborious efforts of coitus and that, in order to discharge their semen, males rise vertically in sudden virile pride, convinced they are fulfilling a superior task, or quite simply to instruct their partners to take their turn.

However, it has been reported that in the Southern Seas, a variety of starfish have recourse to coupling or to a primitive form of coupling, whereby one stretches out and undulates on top of the other, and in their embrace, driven by a momentum that is not their own, they each use the full sensitive army of their feet, which end in suckers. The sensations there must be incredible, unsettling, and intimate, even though, there, too, fertilization continues to be exterior: their offspring develop in the universe of the sea as if sired by it, without incurring any debt or servile gratitude, since all parental attachment has been spared them.

Choreography in the Dark

I am putting the lobster and the crayfish in the same section, for, if they are physically different, they do nevertheless share similar qualities and analogous appetites. Both lead a mostly nocturnal life, opt for the same favorite dishes, enjoy spending their time along rocky coasts, but are sometimes overcome by a sudden mood for migration.

In love, these species also seduce each other with long parades, developing into enigmatic and complicated forms of choreography, ending at last with a similar mating pattern in which the female is on her back, intertwining her feet, her feelers, or her pincers with those of her partner in the so-called missionary position. We shall see what needs to be understood in these "missions" and better yet in these "emissions," but let us start out by saying that the event, displaying inventiveness in the repertoire of lovemaking, opens up novel perspectives in achievement and feeling. This method of breeding or copulation, without having the privilege of being true coitus in due form, is nevertheless beneath the large shimmering mirrors of the sea a rare, perhaps even a unique, thing.

Before we venture further into their libidinous intimacies, let us first identify their physical equality and differences. These large crustaceans live inside a closed carapace, isolated on all sides by a hard chitin covering, wholly inaccessible to emotion one would think. The armor is never taken off and serves at one and the same time as a majestic ornament, a warrior's paraphernalia, and a protective device. Even in love, when contact consists of delicate bumps of their armor, they never know the chance or the charm of nudity: they mate in costume.

The carapace plays the role of a prison that grows larger, however, and expands, and is renewed depending on various moltings, especially during the changes of puberty from which they emerge sexually mature. It is a prison in which they are entirely comfortable beneath a rigid garment that is at first too wide, then is filled with their substance, and in the end will fit exactly to measure. As with the shrimp and the crab, the molt happens through a series of contractions, pushes, lacerations, only to result in a self-liberation at the end of this series of concerted and painful efforts.

Encased like this, one would think them indifferent, cold, frigid, and immune to any emotion, but nothing could be more inaccurate. Though wrapped in a shield, they enjoy a well-developed and sure sense of smell while a nervous and well-extended slender rod allows the sensory spines to capture, register, and decode the subtlest of sensations. This nervous sensitivity, which first of all endows them with a sharp sense of direction, facilitates sophisticated behavior, whether in the capture of prey, in combat, or on parade.

The shell of the crayfish is purplish brown, completely bristling with thorny spines that seem like just so many points of defense stuck in a suit of armor. The lobster's shell, on the other hand, is of one piece, most frequently greenish brown, and has the ability to change hues with its personal moods or circumstances, whether it is a question of lurking in a corner, of hiding in the dark of a crevice, or of appearing in bright daylight with the intention of dazzling the world. In fact, they have a variety of pigments available to them, oranges, purples, greens, or a dark ebony brown, so as to dress appropriately in the purple of passion, the green of austerity, or the deep blue of a kind of royal silence.

The crayfish lacks the powerful pincers the lobster displays with menacing arrogance. On the other hand, it is endowed with antennae that are longer than its body and are useful both in its sensory explorations and in meeting and clasping more tightly in an embrace.

Both species, hindered by an abdomen as large as their appetite, move by walking on the sea bottom in what might be called a disorderly fashion, but they do have the possibility of slapping their tail when faced with danger so as to suddenly retreat. In the course of their nocturnal excursions, they consume the same food with a predilection for mollusks, shellfish, or snails, after which the lobster always goes back to the same shelter, entrenched in the rocks, following an itinerary that lies delineated in his memory.

Both of them sometimes set out on seasonal migrations, sometimes not at all. There is an interior preparation at work, and in the undercurrents of their nervous sensitivity, with growing excitement, they gather in a group under the injunction of sound signals produced by rubbing and bumping their armor. What is the meaning of this massive exile in which they move across the bottom by the thousands in single file, following a leader? What is the reason for this exodus, if not the appeal of a new and promised sea, where they will find their favorite foods in abundance. When you move forward in a stubbornly led procession, connected by invisible bonds to the one in front of you and surely with moments of doubt, of a so-to-speak existential hesitancy of despair and rebellion, you always want to attract the eyes of providence in the struggle, sway it in some way to ensure a superior protection that cannot possibly be defined.

It is again through sound signals that the males, as they explore the territory in search of females, invite them to come out of their rocky refuge. They send out steady calls, sharp and insistent, subtler almost imploring rubbings, scraping slides that resemble those of a bow over a musical saw.

In a swift sharpening of the senses, a stirring of sensitive molecules, passion shakes them at the time of the great tides. That is when physical changes take place, especially among the females, who, upon finding love, want a new outfit, a youthful line, to be the messenger of some novelty for the unknown and transient lover. But doesn't love, even if known only fleetingly, also inscribe living beings in the heart of eternity, which is contained in the wider dimension of the moment? Whether the occasion be a passing fancy or everlasting and faithful, love is always the reconstitution of an original fusion, an initial circle to which the partners bring their complementary abilities, the missing half.

The moon and the light of the stars—the illegible scrawl of luminous bursts twisting and turning, which no inhabitant of the sea ever dreams of deciphering—are bathing the waters in huge bluish shadows, in an ivory shimmer where movements are clad in an enchanted substance, in the reflections and glitter of a magic spell. It is a magic that adds something ghostlike or supernatural, creating at the same time the necessary illusion, the certainty of glory that, although temporary, does not diminish an exceptional moment.

It sometimes happens that several suitors, turning instantly into rivals, meet before the same coveted female. Immediately battles are waged, rather murderous tournaments (among lobsters in particular) that have already been described in the chapter on the crab. I don't know, however, whether lobsters have the same regenerative faculty as crabs or whether they remain mutilated for life.

At last, when the winner alone is left standing, a strange seductive dance begins that captures the female's full attention and fills her whole vision. He exerts himself, rises up, moves his feet, antennae, or pincers at different angles, and leaps up by slapping his tail, sometimes backward, sometimes forward, as he ventures nearer.

In her need to be valued but still entrenched in capricious reserve, she observes him at first with an impassive eye, as one might examine a stack of proposals or deals. Then she seems to be stirred, even marveling at herself slyly, as she feels her resistance melt away and her desire increase.

Her suitor's display is prolonged in a complicated choreography that has some of the qualities of contemporary dance with its spasmodic surges, attacklike holds, pincer gestures that seem like threats, and a wriggling around within himself in which he seeks connection with some inner spring, to release the flow of spontaneous gestures and innovative steps.

He has come closer, close enough to touch her, stroke her, brush against her, awakening all the sensitive areas of his partner one by one, while his hues constantly change and he becomes a kind of kaleidoscopic lobster every time he turns around or shakes his abdomen. When they embrace, their antennae and feet begin to play an important role as they feel their way. It sometimes happens that the male lifts her up and carries her on top of himself, triumphantly, and the fiancée of the moment is delighted to be carried high and borne like a queen across the shifting windows of the sea and the ivory shimmer of the moon. Her genital organs are placed on the ventral side at the last ring of the thorax, while her fiancé has his sexual orifices attached to his last thoracic feet. Since he is deprived of a penis, his feet play the role of copulating organs like a fork and knife playing above a favorite dish. He carries his semen over with a confident movement, as if he had been guided in that motion by the female's nimble finger. It is the same manner of connecting as that of the crab, which we have adequately described in that chapter. Still, it should be clarified that lobsters hold each other with their pincers, while crayfish, with their well-developed and flexible abdominal muscles, connect and embrace with their antennae to clasp each other as closely as possible.

What until now has not been known, the novelty in love relationships among the majority of sea creatures, is that the male, whether lobster or crayfish, turns his partner over on her back to mate with her, in the earlier mentioned, so-called missionary position.

This is no longer the straddling of the crab, the climb from the back, or the piling up while the partners' eyes, shaken by the effort, get lost in the same strange and vague space. Henceforth, facing each other, the bodies fit exactly, fuse like joined palms at the moment of prayer, and seem to be exulting rather than supplicating as they give of themselves.

This new relationship, singularly similar to the habits of humans in the act of love, confers something of a religious significance upon the carnal ceremony by allowing a true intimacy to be shared, the intimacy of facing each other, whereby the original union is renewed with each embrace.

Swimming as a Couple

*P*hysically and with a lack of morality (or might it be a question of an ethics wholly based on self loyalty?), whether in their appetites or in love's fleeting glory, shrimp show most of the characteristics and aptitudes we have seen among the large crustaceans.

Their bodies are more or less colorless and are difficult to see in the water; the cloudy transparency of their outlines is lost among other transparencies where the waves consolidate in a blur around the seaweed undulating in the currents.

But what a miracle when you see them! What a pleasure, when, in contemplation almost, you watch every detail and admire that slender, graceful little body, grown longer, spindly and slight, equipped with long antennae, many feet, and flattened appendages that look like oars or paddles. It swims as if by leaps in the privilege of freedom and inebriation, while others are reduced to walking, to a chaotic, awkward, and rough advance, to sometimes desperate excursions when no prey, whether food or love, appears within reach of their pincers.

Shrimp move in bands along the shores, groups going in the same direction at the mercy of the currents, with an electric mood, so to speak, running through them, changed sometimes into gangs of plunderers venturing into the plankton. When they're taken by surprise, facing danger, a predatory enemy, they turn their abdomen suddenly inward following the example of the lobster and crayfish, moving backward in fits and starts, widening the distance relentlessly. Or else, from their undefined color, they change tone, take on the iridescent hue of the sand or that of the seaweed in which they sway or on which they sit, clutching it, for an indefinite period of time.

The food lover, when deveining them, may notice a small grayish blister, which at first he sees as the sole of a foot or a connecting point. In reality, it is the blind female of the *Bopyrus*, living as a parasite on our little shrimp, while the male of her species has lived on her as a parasite, hooking on to her appendages for security and to satisfy his hunger.

Through its freedom of movement, the shrimp seems to adjust to intruders, perhaps not even noticing their presence, as if it were all a game of transparencies or two-way mirrors. This phenomenon might help us gain insight into and understand when, in our human societies, we see parasitism become outrageously increased as everyone engages in pillage and plunder, occupied by inferior and imitative creations, drawn by a desire that is not their own, going so far as to have a ready-to-wear soul.

In love, shrimp copy the rituals practiced among the other crustaceans. Forms of mating, either straddled like the crab or with the intimacy of a partner turned over on her back, in which case, lacking a penis, the males use their feet as copulating organs to transport the semen to the oily, burning spot. Still, shrimp find their pleasure in swimming, and they use it in lovemaking.

At high tide, they move along below the waves using movements that suddenly seem feverish, electric, and rushed. They swim as you would fly through space, with moments of rising and falling, with U-turns, with drifting glides, which in the air would be the prolonged bursts of full flight.

At the touch of antennae or feet, the females shrink back, anxious at the reaction they feel at this first contact, a stirring of the molecules, an emotion they do their best to contain. Dumbfounded, almost frightened, they watch the parade that is growing under their very eyes, still worried about what too quick a consent might bring in its wake, an impatience that would spoil three-quarters of the pleasure. This is not something they think about, but they do assimilate it instinctively in their fibers. The mind, in its comprehension, would separate them from the world, and it is with the senses that they must be rejoined. To think would be a waste of time and a useless detour when one has almost instant bliss.

Finally, one of the females gives in to the male's invitation, and he then embraces her with his feet, and directed sideways, with a sure tenderness, he takes her off for a swim. The two of them move forward in undulations, with very lively leaps, in a supple repeated release of the abdomen.

In a spare, vigilant, and agile pattern, the water sprites, rubbing but not scraping each other, flow along with the currents, the rush of the waters, the rustle of the loosening foam, and the moods of the sea. The couple ventures into the seaweed's dance, attracted by the glitter and drawn by the fleeting reflections of ivory at night. They cross thresholds we cannot see, hidden passages, they dive into the colder regions and stronger eddies of the great tides. They cross all kinds of turbulence and are jolted and carried away, thereby veering off course. They grant themselves a rest, perched together on a trembling plant, lavishing new caresses on each other, more subtle, intimate, and embracing, before they go back to swimming again, gliding just below the surface indefinitely, sharing the pleasure of feeling themselves in motion, fluid, moving, united, brushed and caressed by the currents.

It is reported that some shrimp give off light. As when fireworks are set off, a sequence of phosphorescent bursts, they illuminate the underwater abysses, enveloping themselves in a brilliant cloud, disguising themselves from every eye, without our knowing whether they seek to be preserved beneath the aura, to be lit up in the adventure, or whether they choose to accomplish the love act in the spotlight, so to speak.

Love in a Seashell

$\mathcal{A}$ shell forces you into a life of seclusion, where you are your own companion, constantly accompanied, carrying a conical house on your back, able to withdraw into it at any moment. This shell is the security of private life, the jail of retreat, of contemplation, and of a modest, undefined pleasure the world does not know. Most of the time, you lead the life of a recluse, locked in upon your secret at nap time, at the time of digestion and of idle dreams, to open only when the appetites awaken or when a sudden restless mood strikes.

These shells come in every form and every design. Secreted by mollusks, forged in limestone with interiors of mother-of-pearl, of misted and smooth mirrors with iridescent reflections, they coil up sometimes eccentrically, sometimes concentrically over a circle, a curve, or a whorl of infinity. They carry projections or shining ridges, are embellished with colors that vary from carmine pink to violet and deep blues, from various ochers and umbers to Veronese and emerald greens. The lyrical abstractions of their fascinating shapes are demarcated, punctuated by light tones and black lines, sometimes with a puzzling calligraphy, which is surely that of ancient times.

We can see that these mollusks have a taste for marvelously decorating their personal prison, which is no longer or is less a prison when its living conditions are accepted, without losing one's soul therein, to use the maxim expressed by Baudelaire in *Les Paradis artificiels*. The fact remains that, as a useless pleasure, these aesthetics have a dangerous audacity and an inconsistent approach. For in the end, if lackluster, they would be better concealed from lustful gazes, and, by forgoing their baroque ridges and projections, they would offer less of a grip. There again, we have examples where nature, forgetting the price of life and security, strives hard to create extravagant forms, to unreservedly compose with colors in a spirit of pure disinterest, a bold desire for beauty. The thing, brought to a point of luxury, wealth, and sophistication far beyond any predator's power of appreciation, forces us to understand that all seduction is self-motivated to start with: one must please oneself in order to gain the necessary esteem.

Seashells are basically identified as two kinds: either they consist of two valves, joined by a muscular hinge; or they are molded as if cast from one form. In love, in the first case, the fertilization remains exterior through private secretions entrusted to the currents' whims. In the other case, the invention of the penis opens the field to all sorts of unique incongruities and inspirations, all the way to the pattern of hermaphroditism, whereby one penetrates the other and is at the same time penetrated by him, instantly experiencing that which he experiences.

Cockles, Razor Shells, Scallops
Among these species, the hinge connects the two valves of the compartment, without limiting their movements when swimming, jumping, or burrowing. The mantle secretes the shell with a material it has prepared inside itself; as time goes by, the shell is decorated with rings of growth like necklaces that attest to puberty, maturity, and then to a tranquil wisdom or an indifferent gloom.

These bivalves have a pallial chamber where the respiratory branchiae are, edged with cilia that make the current inside circulate. They also feed by filtering microorganisms of plankton, brought in by the water running through them, as the entrance and exit orifices are close to each other.

Depending on the tides, cockles, rising from nowhere and everywhere, are washed up on the shore, on the sometimes sandy, sometimes gritty, beach of the moment. This is the end of a mad journey and the beginning of something else. Their shells, which served as primitive currency, are adorned with radiating projections, the ridges of each valve fanning out to the edge.

The mantle is lengthened by a highly developed foot that ends in a curved point. The cockle uses it both to burrow under and to move ahead in a somewhat disorganized manner, like a ballerina who is an eternal beginner and wobbles on her toe shoes. Yet, it has an elegant way of showing its foot, of looking for a rough patch to hook onto, to contract, and then to propel itself about a hand's length forward.

In order to burrow under, again using its foot, it digs, scrapes, whittles, and discards debris, through a series of muscle stretches and contractions, all rather quickly, until it disappears entirely in the crunching somnolence of the sand, as if in a loss of consciousness, a recurrent oblivion of the world and perhaps of itself as well. The razor shell shares this delight in burrowing; it, too, makes use of its expanded foot, retracts it, then expands it once more, taking the rest of its shell with it in jerking motions.

The scallop, on the other hand, develops a rather astounding swimming technique. It lies quietly on the sea bottom, tranquilly indifferent in a moment of blissful abandon with its shell just slightly open. Suddenly, faced with danger, when a starfish or an octopus approaches, or when seized by sudden wanderlust, it roughly shuts its valves, inverts the flow of water in its pallial chamber and thus manages to propel itself forward. Repeating the operation, it swims in fits and starts with jaunty leaps at a speed that doesn't seem to tire it out, as it is so accustomed to it. A series of deep blue eyes lies at the edge of the pallial cavity, and these allow it to detect deep shadows and great brightness in its path as soon as it opens its valves again.

All these bivalve species are either male or female, first dispersing their gametes through an orifice that is situated in the pallial chamber. The long cilia of the branchiae move around making the water inside circulate, thereby driving their seed out. The whole business is rather practical. But it is, once again, an anonymous form of love, practiced sullenly and without enthusiasm, the way you fulfill an obligation or send mail off without specifying the name of the addressee. Fertilization takes place haphazardly, where currents intersect, where they have no business, where there is nobody around. It is as if you were to throw bottles into the sea indifferently, bottles without any message, except for the one that is similarly inscribed in all beings from the time of their conception and that forms the program of their basic flowering.

Limpets and Winkles, Trochus or Whelks

Invention and all kinds of perfected forms of affection are produced in marine gastropods—the winkle, the limpet, the Trochus or the whelk—whose shells are fashioned out of a single piece, rolled and turned like a helix.

Fertilization in becoming internal, with the appearance of the penis, opened the field for true relationships with innumerable interactions, a repertoire of caresses and lengthy foreplay that serve to awaken and sharpen the senses. Finally, distance was shattered, the relationship became less anonymous through contact and penetration; love is made in the undefined and familiar spaces of sensitivity, through the indescribable variety of bonding in a complete or almost complete intimacy.

The same words return and seek to compose themselves in close arching circles in trying to describe the shell of a gastropod based on a spiral, a curve that draws revolutions around a fixed point growing wider each time. The spiral has the fascination of an archaic, archetypal motif; a sign of the origins, a basic and obvious secret; perhaps it is even a question of imagining the development of our own destiny.

These species have the ability to withdraw entirely inside their shell, to fuse with rocks as limpets do or, like whelks, to close in upon themselves with their seal of horned or limestone material. They move by means of a flattened foot shaped like a plump disk that allows for continuous gliding.

Their advance is enthralling in its consummate art of ease and calm assurance. They progress in time, a time that is theirs, a time no longer flowing in the same rhythm. They lag behind, shrink back, stretch, and crawl as they advance with concerted movements. Lengthy shivers go through their foot, surges created by a series of muscle contractions. In a mechanism anointed by their mood, an extension followed by a tightening of the parallel folds is produced, a series of contractions followed by a wider stretch. They walk around with their shell bouncing from one side to the other, find their direction, hug the contours, go around the obstacle of a pebble, lubricating their progress as they go along.

Sometimes when they are faced with danger, such as a crack in the terrain like a collapsed road, they rise up and roll their horns in incomprehension or bewilderment. They withdraw halfway beneath their shell, exude more slime, carefully come back out again, folding back their eye stems to size themselves up once more as well as the world around them. Then they begin to make their way again sideways, purposefully, going back to the pastures of their everyday gluttony.

To feed themselves, these species most often graze the tiny seaweed covering the rocks, using a radula, an agile band bearing tiny even-sized teeth set in rows, that functions like a grater. Once this somewhat austere banquet is ended, the limpet, loyal to its favorite spot, returns to its original location before low tide. It retraces its steps, finds its imprint, the round engraved nest, into which it fits perfectly once again, securing itself with a kind of glue secreted by the foot: then it can resist every attack and all harm from wave and undertow.

When love begins to burn their senses, they must go out, go out immediately, with more diligence and less prudence, go back into the world, secreting trails of slime behind them in order to find themselves and recompose themselves alone after the adventure. There is a kind of rush, of rejoicing in

moving along, as if they might miss a rendezvous, an occasion that might never come along again.

Crossing familiar perimeters, they venture farther, where
they have never gone before, where they no longer have reference points. As soon as they see each other, they immediately recognize their own desire reflected in the other as if
everything, right away, were enacted in a mirror and dou-
bled. The ceremony will be conducted under a reign of pro-
crastination, of time drawn out, of pleasant laziness, in
which attraction and the complicity of affection are, nevertheless, instantaneous. All around them, the world of the
sea is moving, undulating, and resplendent, breaking as if
through facets of liquid crystal.

They approach each other on a long and voluptuous col-
lision course. But before they roll on their sides and come
close enough to face each other and adjust their fleshy feet,
and indeed secure them with the froth they secrete through
the play of their adorned suction pads, they abandon themselves to foreplay. A thousand touches. The shells sway. The
horns collide gently and intertwine delicately. They feel
each other with their long peduncles, almost intertwining,
so close to their eyes.

Already they are kissing and nibbling at each other's
throats. Since their tongue is a radula covered with thousands of rough spots, these kisses are cruel and delicious.
When you are a mollusk, with a very slow-moving nature,
simple touches and more knowledgeable caresses are not
enough to kindle the love act. Inflicting sharp and insis-

tent pain, repeated several times in the same spot or in a continued line, they arouse the whole geography of the sensitive, the map of their erotic receptivity, as if they were tracing the borders within which their double and mutual embrace will soon occur. As they roll along they hug each other, enfold each other, come apart frothing abundantly, and then clutch each other even more tightly with reciprocal suction. They end up uniting in a ritual in which the sexes mingle and interact in several inventive ways.

Among the lower gastropods and among the bivalves fertilization continues to occur outside through the random encounter of their private secretions. Organically, the gametes emerge through an orifice in the pallial chamber from which agitated cilia soon expel them into the exiting current. Among sea snails something innovative has happened, where a groove lengthens the mantle cavity to its entrance. In this location a penis could gradually appear and develop, first of a disproportionate size, with hooks, points, or scales, from lack of confidence in its effectiveness. Confronted with this marvel, the females came to the point of taking their genital organs out completely only to withdraw them later, once impregnation or the capturing of semen had taken place.

The sea snail has been doubly equipped. The females being endowed with a penis and the males with an oily receiving groove, our gastropods created or re-created the pattern of hermaphroditism, as they mate in two ways at one and the same time. They embrace each other or place themselves head to foot, "one penetrating the other and being penetrated by the other at the same time, feeling the pleasure he provides at the same moment he obtains it."

The appearance of the penis profoundly changed love relationships and, indeed, truly established them by opening them up to a variety of visions. Nevertheless, it should be noted that this penis was not always located in a convenient place, as it is among the developed species today. It seems that nature first struggled blindly, proceeding with all kinds of attempts that ended in surprising and preposterous results, to the extent that the tool has sometimes been seen to project from the throat, sometimes to stick out in the area of the eye, and even to protrude from the mouth of the partners.

In reciprocal copulation, where one behaves both as male and female, some also go so far as to make use of a thin limestone stylet, known as the "love spear," which they set into each other's flesh with the purpose of arousing excitement and inciting an immediate riot of the senses when nature moves too slowly. It is also reported that, with the novelty of the equipment, they go so far as to make love in a chain. A female is always the leader; the others function as males to the one in front and give themselves as females to the one behind. We are seeing here a primitive orgy, debauchery that doesn't have the merit of being immoral and, because of that, lacks spice and minimizes real enthusiasm for the task.

The fact remains, however, that in their double embrace, which is never a mirrored relationship but a true double exchange, our gastropods rediscover the original fusion; the impossible and double identity has finally been re-created. All imagination is useless, all fantasy is superfluous, when the reciprocal thrust shares the same desire and the same tendencies.

The Seaweed's Dance

*B*eing seaweed offers a rather untroubled existence, a simple arrangement in which you do not move on your own. The body, or what takes its place, let's say its physical aspect, is oddly composed of a group of ribbons made of rubbery material with a brownish hue, with bulges here and there, air-filled blisters, playing the role of floaters.

We lead a fixed existence clinging to the shore's rocks, which are submerged at high tide and lie bare at low tide, thus metronomically dividing time into two primitive periods.

Without ever having concerns about employment or any obligation to get to work, we live off the water that bathes us, assimilating through chlorophyll the carbon dioxide dissolved beneath the waves; little energy is needed when you aren't very active. The currents drive us, direct us, put us down, raise us up, and make us sway beautifully in our only moment of glory. Sometimes, beneath a ground swell, in a fury that remains foreign and over-whelming, we are torn away from the bottom, roughly thrown onto the shore in a heap where, gathered up by human hands, we serve as fertilizer in the fields, as rubber bands for tying up lobsters, or as decoration in the bottom of oyster crates. In slow asphyxiation, a death struggle that bothers no one, this end is as good as any other; it even offers a kind of nobility in the ultimate possibility of being useful to something or someone.

Under names that have been attributed to us, like fucus, kelp, or wrack, we vegetate without languishing, always growing and proliferating. At low tide, we can be found flopped about, more or less wound into a ball, tangled, scat-tered, strewn over the rocks like thick locks of hair. As if coming out of some torpor, we awaken beneath the spatters and the rolling of the waves that return first in crests, then, beneath the cry of seagulls, in the invincible surge of an assault carried ever forward. The sea gives us back a life of motion, the sea brings us back to the dance, playing with us, entwining us, and raising us up in a choreography of undu-lations and swayings impossible to describe, and these are, have no doubt about it, a modest form of voluptuousness. It is the simple pleasure, unambiguous and yet never the same, of being alive and in motion, here and now.

Life first appeared in the primitive ocean in the form of blue algae and bacteria. We are therefore a founding ele-ment of the myth; we are graceful forms from the origins that prevail, that endure in the present, and by which each of us, in the crucible of oneself, is brought back to the spark of the beginning, with the sharpened and sharp desire to start living this life.

Love happens without our even dreaming about it or becoming aware of it. Our sexuality is a program that unfolds entirely on its own, inside us and at the same time outside of us, without asking for our cooperation. We feel no trembling at all, except perhaps when the buds that swell up at the remotest end of our branches begin to grow: it is not a very troubling sensation; rather the cause of a simple joy, of something agreeable being added.

These buds, which are reproductive balls also known as "conceptacles," minuscule and monastic places of conception, are organized into cavities, some containing male and others female cells. The latter give off a brown liquid, while the male cells produce an orange-colored substance, a kind of fairly liquid honey in which the gametes can be discerned: infinitesimal bodies that move briskly thanks to two swimming cilia.

As the buds and these substances mature, it is as though a partition suddenly gives way, a curtain is raised: the male gametes rush ahead to meet their partners, assaulting them from every angle in order to reconstitute a whole. These eggs, after they have developed and fallen to the bottom of the sea, will quickly attach their fronds with clinging tendrils and join the undulating choreography of fully grown seaweed when the tide returns.

Nostalgia for Origins

When you are accustomed to inventive foreplay, to the exchange of caresses and many forms of contact, to all the sensitive delights of the conspiring partner, it is better not to become a salmon.

But if you have an adventurous heart, a liking for great migrations, an obsession for original sources, then you will find your tendencies satisfied with this species. As if you were being carried off on an odyssey with its perils and rites, its exploits and pleasures drawn from the unknown, and all arranged according to a voyage of initiation that ends by coming back to itself, as it turns out.

Salmon are born in winter upstream in rivers and streams. At a tender age they are minuscule individuals, carrying a purse filled with nutrient saps on their abdomen, the vitelline cell, from which they feed while they remain hidden in the gravel and the darkness of the spawning bed.

At that time, furthermore, they benefit from the characteristic of being transparent (the spine barely outlined in crystal), so that predators cannot see them in the clarity of the
water in which a thousand windows become endlessly
entangled as they scatter reflections, moving lights and
shadows in the fleeting perspective of these two-way mirrors. However, the river plays its magic spell only when they
find it the same and yet changed, laden with a familiar
strangeness, bearing the images and scents with which it has
impregnated their memory.

In adolescence, they begin to feed on the larvae of drag-
onflies or water beetles, freshwater shrimp, and small fry,
and are clothed in a grayish gown, ocellated with black dots
and lined with blackish marks: is it a new attribute to help
them blend with the pebble bed among the reflections of
the branches on the surface?

One or two years later, always in springtime, which
imposes itself like an invitation that one wouldn't dream of
resisting, when a bright-silver reflection gradually appears
in their scales, the salmon gather in groups, meet in schools,
in the joy of coming close, with a boldness that is aug-
mented by the crowd and the excitement of the approach-
ing departure.

They flash a thousand silvery sparkles through the waves,
swim in all directions before they orient themselves, and
then reunited in the direction of the current, of the
unknown, and of the great adventure, they let themselves
be carried off, commended to the same transparent force

that engendered them, and start their descent toward the sea. They cross waterfalls, bound in angels' leaps, grow intoxicated with forbidden sensations in the falls and swirls of foam. They skirt cold shadows, cross sunlit sections, fields of light and reflections, before they are again swept away and dragged in rapids, beneath cracks, in an explosion of light. Farther down, they reassemble, thanks to a slower course, in an ever-shimmering procession, a silky parade, until at last they reach the mouth of the river where the waves forcefully drive them back.

The water whirls in the estuary, rolls up and back, is unleashed in broken circles, tugged at by opposite currents, and they, in spite of their efforts, in spite of a hundred attempts, cannot cross this turbulent barrier.

For an indefinite period of time, they stay there, captive in the water's lap, the moving space of their waiting, as they limber up their muscles, gaining strength, bolstering their resolution to be tested, to succeed at last in prevailing over the power of the sea. They clear the barrier, emerge in the enormous space of conquest, pulled along by broad currents, by narrow currents without, however, venturing into the deep.

The salmon embark on a magnificent odyssey that never seems to end; they thrust themselves on grand journeys, wanderings in large numbers, interminable crossings, until they come up against unknown shores and linger in the vicinity of islands jutting out of the ocean. Though their flanks are still silvery, a bluish glow now colors their spine like a consecration. They feed on herring, sticklebacks, and crustaceans and then continue on their adventurous journey. They seem to be in quest of an unreachable star, involved in a dream without end, never countering their momentum with boundaries or limitations.

Some salmon choose to pursue their roaming indefinitely without ever returning to spawn in the river where they were born. Is it nature's wisdom to divide them for some reason we cannot comprehend? Is it in the spirit of a whim, of a calling discovered en route? Or is it a determination of personal temperament, so to speak, a destiny to which they submit and which they invent at the same time?

The fact remains that the majority, through an internal signal, a command that echoes in the flesh, initiate the migration of the spawning season, the slow and long return across thousands of miles back to their native waters. They move along at a swift pace, like naked knife blades, swimming in a magnetic billowing, as one takes over from the others, pulled along in a sinuous furrow. Time no longer passes in the same rhythm; they drift in an evasive and interminable infinity, always directly on course, filled with hope and impatience, as if they had to catch up on a delay of their own making, no longer thinking about feeding.

Near the shore, the scent of their native waters, imprinted in their memory, acts like a landmark, but the secret of their sense of direction in the open sea remains unknown. One would have to approach a mysterious force, make an effort to understand it according to the laws of magnetic fields or to the rules of divination, to define, to evaluate the physical reality of this astounding power of attraction. Already they are going back up against the current, confronting waterfalls, riverbed projections where water floods and breaks on the cutting edges of rocks beneath a fury of foam, gouging their entrails with broken glass. They clear waterfalls with dizzying leaps, flights of an unprecedented and fiery spirit in which their bodies coil up, then stretch out and slam in the air.

Upriver, they find the waters of their childhood again, those transparent and icy waters, rolling across the gravel of the spawning bed. Through a sentiment that one might call Oedipal, if seen from a basic and broad angle, they are viscerally attached to the river that engendered them and not to parents, of whom they remember nothing, offering the advantage of a freedom that need be neither grateful nor guilt-ridden. In returning to their origins, as in a ritual repeated to ensure eternal renewal, it is in these places and in these familiar places only, the olfactory imprint of which they carry in their memory, that they choose to reproduce.

Although their great migratory course has exhausted them and made them lean, they instantly forget all their muscular aches and the psychological trials of an interminable journey in order to prepare immediately for the feast of love.

Each female is escorted by several males who sway in place by evenly moving their fins and who watch her as she goes through a series of odd advances. She descends to the

bottom, rubs her belly with industrious and almost voluptuous conviction in the bed of gravel and stones, goes back
and attacks it with violent blows of her tail, thereby digging
the nest in which she will deposit her eggs. The males have
now seen enough and begin fighting each other for the privilege of inseminating her.

Hotheadedly, they wage battles and throw themselves
into contests composed of a series of attacks and reversals of
unbelievable cruelty. They assault each other with their
jaws open, baring rows of sharp teeth to grab each other in
the flank, curl up, stretch out, lash each other with blows of
their tails, scratch each other with strikes of suddenly sharp
fins. The fury intensifies and becomes less controlled. The
courage they display, despite the blows they receive,
increases their ardor, the compelling perspective of the glo-
rious role the conqueror will have to play next. They romp
about in a wildly aggressive war dance, which at moments is
strangely accompanied by short aberrations of a kind of love
parade or seductive gestures, intended only for the eyes of
the female.

She obviously pairs up with the one who emerges from
these battles as the champion, her nature not allowing
another choice. Her partner will relieve himself of his milt
on her eggs with dignity and regal superiority as if he were
part of a coronation ceremony, while she feels a rush of
comfort and contentment in seeing her offering honored.

A patriarch may sometimes allow a few young, still ado-
lescent salmon to accompany him and to imitate his act of

fertilization. In the words of Remy de Gourmont, fish would thus have a kind of schooling in which the experienced teach the processes of procreation to life's newcomers. Better yet one could speak of an initiation in the discovery of self and one's characteristics, through a whole set of teachings and practical exercises.

Then, to protect their offspring, the two partners cover up the eggs with gravel by delicately slapping their tails or by pushing the pebbles with the end of their jaws. And that is the only moment they find themselves even remotely close, always preserving chastity and a lack of contact in their relationship. Still, it is a strange kind of love in which even the rudiments of voluptuousness remain unknown to them, in which they never know the joy of possessing and being possessed, the double delight of seducing the other at the same moment that one is being seduced.

AT THE END OF THE DAY, WE HAD GONE DOWN TO THE inlets of the untamed coast. It was low tide and the seagulls were scattering toward the open sea. Anne-Charlotte was walking ahead of me, offering me a casual view of a touching, rather tiny behind dancing beneath the folds of her skirt. Her blue boots were making gentle hissing noises filling the space between my temples.

She had arrived unexpectedly on the weekend to make sure everything was going well. At the time and rather foolishly, I had the fleeting impression of having been caught guilty or held hostage, sequestered in a house that had been kindly lent to me. Not knowing her too well, I was observing this woman of about forty, with her emaciated face, her sometimes staring sometimes furtive eyes, and her abundant head of hair, acquired through an operation known as "voluminizing the hair," some of the locks bleached, adding an almost silver gray aura. Anne-Charlotte was dressed in long sweaters and woolen skirts that blunted her shape as they enfolded her from shoulder to ankle like a cocoon. Perhaps hiding what would usually be unveiled for approval should be seen as the longing of some women to be loved for what they are, and not for their charms and the "contemptible" pleasure that might be stolen from them. She was coming out of a divorce and far from reinvesting in a new amorous attachment.

The sea was shimmering in the distance with shifting veins of marble, large darker grooves, and a field of glitter around the reefs. A cormorant, dark against the sunlight, dived into the sea in search of prey, or a reflection of himself, Anne-Charlotte said to me.

I was carrying a canvas bag on my shoulder and was surprised by its weight, since all I had put in it was a bottle of water, my pipe and tobacco, and two sweatshirts for when the coastal wind grew cooler. The rocks, covered with rust-colored and golden lichen, were gleaming in the slanting sun, laden with rebus puzzles impossible to decipher, cryptograms engraved by salty winds, calligraphic shapes mixed with droppings of seabirds.

Anne-Charlotte had stopped and was leaning against a rock hewn into a dolmen-shaped table by erosion. Just as she turned around and I saw her open her mouth as if a flow of words were going to carry her off, I suddenly interrupted her with a huge shhhh!, index finger on my lips. Taken aback for a moment, she was looking at me, almost offended or in shock. But as she came down to the bottom of the rocks where the necklaces of foam were coming undone, she was almost smiling, looking amused.

She waved at a group of passing seagulls, which then dispersed, carried off by invisible whirlwinds. The sea spray beading her face made her eyes sparkle like glass. I was happy to see her liberated, as if delivered from the past for a little while. Anne-Charlotte was hopping from one stone to another with the nimbleness of a young goat, having entered into the present moment. She had started to collect mussels, choosing the fattest ones, tearing their anchoring threads with a swift frenzy, the gesture of a child silently gathering, amassing booty. Mussels, but oysters, too, and winkles clustered in a colony of black shells.

Without thinking, as if it were a treasure hunt and we were becoming the greatest predators on the shore, I had followed her example, looking for other seafood in the large transparent puddles the tide had left between the rocks. I found whelks, cockles, and a few sea urchins. Limpets were clinging to the rocks with a kind of glue secreted by their feet, and I was doing my utmost to loosen them, fiddling with my pocketknife until the blade broke and I continued with the stump.

We brought our ever more abundant harvest close to the dolmen-shaped rock table, but Anne-Charlotte did not spread it out on the table and so neither did I. We were entering into a ceremony of which she became the celebrant, her face now full of an almost religious or pagan solemnity, her hair tangled across her face by the rushes of wind returning over the breakers.

I was stunned to see Anne-Charlotte bend over to grab the canvas bag and, with a conjurer's gesture, take out, one after the other, a lace-edged tablecloth, two candlesticks, a bottle of white wine, lemons, oyster knives, and two wine glasses wrapped in a napkin. What, unbeknownst to me, she had added to the bag explained its extra weight. This bit of gear for a somewhat outdated and romantic garden party amazed me, and it didn't occur to me to make fun of her now that I was involved in the ritual. As the shadows were growing longer, all of a sudden turning colder and bluer, I only suggested she put on her sweatshirt, and I did the same, slipping it on and mussing up my hair.

The mirror of the sea was darkening with deeper lines of marbling, wide furrows of ink that, by contrast, endowed the foam with a snowy gleam, a glassy shimmering on the crest of the waves, a color of white grapes like crushed crystal. Anne-Charlotte laid out the collected shells on the tablecloth in an order that was impossible to grasp, an intuitive harmony peculiar to her, as ornamentation, the importance being in the presentation. She continued without worrying about the stains she was making. And maybe it even pleased her to see them appear, these sticky marks, these stains of the sea's moods that were widening into moist shadows in the fabric, while her own fingers were getting wet, covered with a kind of rust.

It was my task to light the candles with my lighter and to light them again when the wind, getting lost in the reefs, would blow them out. Their glow played on our faces as in a Georges de La Tour painting, adding the delicate substance of mystery, of mysticism even, or of a strange intimacy, while the evening was falling like fabric on the moving patches of the ocean. We had raised our glasses, making a wordless toast to the whole world and, without doubt, to ourselves in the first place.

Anne-Charlotte had the gleam of a challenge in her eyes. One of those provocative looks by which you let someone close know that you see him as incapable of daring to do anything. Or perhaps she was only looking for acceptance in my eyes, for an absolute response or a conspiracy both serious and playful.

She had first picked up one of the limpets that I had loosened from the rock and, not taking her eyes off me, had nibbled it with her teeth and then chewed the flesh, which was actually rather tough. With the palm of her hand over her mouth for a moment, as if to keep from throwing up, she went back to chewing a pulp streaked with the thin bits of shell that were crunching between her teeth. A dam had burst within her. Huge crystal-clear tears were rolling down her cheeks, and she wasn't trying to hold them in or wipe them away with the back of her hand. They were almost tears of joy or of released jubilation in which she couldn't yet believe, in a moment of solace or shameful hedonism.

Watching her, I felt enormously stirred and gripped; but I didn't want to be outdone, be just a witness or, worse, a voyeur. I grabbed a first shell, then another, opening mussels and oysters on the tablecloth, ever more soaked with the sea's secretions. Skillfully I cut apart the five reddish parts lying star-shaped on the lower part of the sea urchin. All this was to be tasted while squeezing quarters of lemon over them. All this was to be nibbled and swallowed as salty water seeped into the corners of our mouths. We were opening other shells, loosening the strange-looking flesh with the point of the blade, gleaming fruits, mysterious, intimate with the moist secret of ancient origins. These were fruits to indulge in, and we indulged in them, swallowing without chewing, or chewing lengthily before swallowing the fluid forms, smooth, icy and salty, delights of sensitive life withdrawing on our lips and then expanding again inside the darkness of our mouths, handed over to our taste buds, delivered to glassfuls of white wine.

Without saying a word, in the vacillating brightness of the candles, we continued the banquet, *our* banquet, our bodies bent forward, motionless, at the table, but swaying and supple like seaweed inside ourselves. It was as if we had grown at our fingertips and our temples, predatory pincers, antennae, tentacles with which to open the shells, to force them to open by pressure while playing at the same time with our short-bladed knives, wedged in the palms of our hands.

Undoubtedly, one never becomes other than what one eats. But in feeding off this seafood until we were no longer thirsty, until we were beyond hunger, borne away, carried off in a jubilant and irrepressible movement surpassing all normal appetites, were we also and at the same time going to swallow and assimilate their specific characteristics, their ways of moving, their processional dances, the hermaphroditic privileges of the gastropods, the private secretions of the sea urchins? Leaving this feast, which looked more and more like the carnage of sensual pleasure, were we going to be endowed with new powers?

As Anne-Charlotte was opening one last oyster shell, inserting the knife point in its side, she cut herself near her thumb. She was handing me the shell on which a little of her scarlet blood had fallen with something like an expectant look in her eyes, something imperturbable, an almost imperceptible insistence. After a very short moment of indecision, feeling a void inside me, I brought it to my mouth while the triangular and straight flames of the candles stopped the shadows around us from moving.